KEEP IT $IMPLE $TUPID

How to Protect Your Finances from Wall Street and Yourself

RICHARD TIMOTHY
CURRAN, JD, CFP®

To Wynne, Cole and Brenna – the best part of my life, always
Never forget that I love you and that life is a journey... IZWATITZ

Special thanks to: Wynne, Jeff, Mick, Zimbo, Russ,
Dingle, Megan, Nanno, Dave, Dick, Adam, Chip.
– I appreciate all your time and input!

All royalties to be donated to the Carolinas ALS Research Fund
to help fight Lou Gehrig's Disease.

Contents

Preface

When I was in law school (yes, I am a proud yet reformed lawyer), I was told that the simpler I made my argument, the more potential for understanding. "Tim," my professor said, "Remember this: keep it simple stupid."

After realizing that he was not actually calling me stupid, I figured out that this was more than a simple way to remember an important concept.

The KISS theory, as it is known, is a philosophy that stresses that the simpler something is, the better it is. Unfortunately, we human beings have an innate ability to make everything more complicated. Part of the curse of having cognitive ability is being able to take something very simple and over analyze it.

So I decided to write an investment book that clearly, and simply, conveys what you need to know, what you need to avoid, and how to apply these lessons in real life. You see, there are far too many books born from academia that lose their usefulness by just engulfing the reader in all sorts of statistics and theories.

This book, in contrast, was forged out of real life. To wit, I am not a professor. I am not a research analyst. I am not a statistician. I am, however, someone who has worked with real, live people for well over twenty years, helping construct investment portfolios and retirement plans as well as give comprehensive financial advice.

I am an attorney who practiced law back in the 1990s. I am a CERTIFIED FINANCIAL PLANNER™ (CFP®) who manages a good bit of money for individuals. I am also an industry arbitrator for the Financial Industry Regulatory Authority (FINRA).

I started my career at A.G. Edwards and Sons as a financial advisor. After becoming a Vice President of Investments, I decided to transfer to PaineWebber Securities, which became UBS Financial Services. While at UBS, I was not only a Vice President of Investments, but a Senior Retirement Planning Consultant as well.

In 2003, however, I left the wirehouse brokerage system and started my own financial planning and asset management practice, called TWC Wealth Management, LLC, located in Charlotte, North Carolina. My wife Wynne (a financial advisor as well) and I are known as The Finance Couple™.

I also wanted to write this book because I believe the investing public has not been educated well enough by Wall Street – yet the investing public is not as ignorant as my industry would try to have them believe. You see, most of Wall Street thinks that the less the public knows, the easier it is to sell them something.

But the investing public must take some blame as well, if for nothing else than being lazy. So, this book will not only teach you what you need to know, but it will also prod you to take some action – because only you can take control of your financial destiny.

In keeping with the KISS premise, I will not bore you with irrelevant rhetoric (as a universal cynic, I believe too many books, especially instructional ones like this, could be cut in half without losing any of their usefulness). I will only point out the most important issues and how to tackle them using logic and common sense (which is terribly uncommon these days!).

I will also give you a "behind-the-scenes" glimpse into my industry; an industry that I am proud to be part of, yet embarrassed by the shenanigans that occur. By doing so, you will be better equipped to steer clear of people, products and/ or strategies that are ultimately unimportant, potentially detrimental, and definitely a hindrance to your success.

Last, but not least, please remember this book is not meant to be a complete personal financial plan, but rather a crucial guide, or roadmap, as you steer towards financial success. Since you're different than everyone else in so many ways, your financial plan and accompanying strategies must be tailored to your specific situation; no book can dictate exactly what *you* should do in every circumstance.

So, with that being said, let's get started!

Chapter 1

Save Yourself from Yourself

"Where we have strong emotions,
we're liable to fool ourselves."
– Carl Sagan

Let's assume you bought 100 shares of a stock for $40 per share (cost = $4000), and less than nine months later it's trading for $80 per share (current value = $8000). Your first reaction might be something like, "Wow! What a great stock! I'm glad I was smart enough to buy it before it doubled in price." But after potentially convincing yourself that you are a great stock investor comes the hard part: now you have to decide what to do with that stock. Do you hold onto it, hoping for more gains? Or do you sell it, thinking you may have gotten lucky and just want to savor your winnings?

Another alternative might be to essentially do both; you could sell half of the stock and hold onto the other half. By taking this approach, you not only might get back your original investment (less any transaction costs, of course), but you also still own some of the stock – and if it continues to go up, then great, but if it goes down, then at least your original investment is not in jeopardy. Unfortunately, I don't think too many people consider this alternative; instead, fear and greed might cause most people to only consider whether to buy (more) or sell the stock, which may not be the most rational choice.

Fear and greed, the two most prominent emotions when it comes to finance; people think they will either lose money (fear) or miss out on some great opportunity (greed). Everyone has made mistakes with their finances, sometimes huge mistakes, and nine times out of ten it comes down to a bad decision based on fear or greed.

Now, before I go any further, I would be remiss if I did not remind you again that I am a financial planner who has worked in this business for over twenty years. So you may think I have a bias, which is fair.

But this in no way diminishes the first point of this book: **you need someone to give you objective input on your finances!** Because the only way to remove fear and greed is to get help from someone that is not emotionally connected to your money.

Sure, you can kid yourself that you are able to disassociate all emotion from your financial decisions. But just remember that your finances are not unlike your children. No matter how hard you try to make an objective, non-biased decision regarding your child, deep down you can never forget that the decision affects your child – and thus your heart-strings get tugged whether you like it not.

It doesn't matter how much or how little you have, or how smart you may be about finances, the simple truth is that you are

emotionally connected to your money, and thus fear and greed will play a part in every decision you make about your money. This is why so many people screw up their finances, which includes their financial plan or lack thereof, as well as their portfolio - because they do not get help from someone that's emotionally unattached to their money.

Now, I am not advocating that everyone should run out and hire me or some other financial advisor. And I am not saying that you cannot do this yourself. In fact, I believe you   do this yourself – *if* you treat it like the full-time job that it is (which most people do not have time or patience for), *and* you periodically get an outside, objective opinion on what you are doing.

Another good reason to work with someone is to make sure you have a succession plan in place. I can't tell you how many couples I've talked to where one spouse has an interest in finance and the other does not. The risk is when, not if, the one with the interest gets sick or passes away, and then the surviving spouse that has no interest will be a sitting duck for some financial salesperson.

Regardless of whether you get someone to help you or not, this book is all about getting you to help yourself. So if you go it alone, that's fine, the lessons in this book are intended to help guide you to a more successful financial life either way.

But if you do hire someone, then please, please…

Chapter 2

Beware of Financial Advisors in Sheep's Clothing

*"It is a tale told by an idiot,
full of sound and fury, signifying nothing."*
– William Shakespeare

There are a lot of good "financial advisors" out there. The tough part is finding an experienced one that is competent *and* unencumbered by conflicts of interest.

Although there are a lot of qualified advisors, too many of them practice their profession from within a system that is riddled with conflicts. You see, if an advisor works as an employee of a bank or brokerage firm, then their primary loyalty typically is to that employer, and thus not to you. Accordingly, if an advisor who is an employee of a bank or brokerage firm tells you that they only work for your best interest, they may be kidding themselves, and, more importantly, you as well.

As for potentially incompetent or sales-driven advisors (understanding that every industry in the world might have good, bad or indifferent participants), it can be harder to discern who belongs in these categories, and most industry titles may offer little help. For instance, have you noticed how most people connected to the finance industry, regardless of whether they just sell insurance products or simply manage assets (as opposed to offering comprehensive financial advice), seem to be called a "financial advisor"? In my opinion, this title has been so bastardized that it means literally nothing other than the fact that the person works in personal finance; it may carry absolutely no credibility in and of itself.

Similarly, just because an advisor has a title like "Vice President" does not necessarily mean they are good at what they do. It could just mean they generate a lot of money for their employer by gathering a lot of assets. But just because they are good at gathering assets does not mean they actually know their asses from their elbows when it comes to dispensing financial advice!

To add insult to injury, if an advisor spends the majority of their time trying to gather new assets, then their current clients probably suffer from lack of attention.

There are, however, some titles that I believe may convey some competence. Those titles include CERTIFIED FINANCIAL PLANNER™ (or CFP®) and Chartered Financial Analyst or Consultant (ChFC®) – both of which require substantial time and effort to receive. But there are too many other titles that can be had for minimal studying and a fee. And if a title is too easy to get, then it probably doesn't mean much at all, except that the advisor wants to add some symbols behind his or her name to seemingly look smarter than they otherwise may be.

You should also avoid pure salespeople, who may account for a good deal of so-called "financial advisors". These salespeople may come in the form of insurance agents, asset gatherers, or other advisors who might try to peddle one product or another in hopes of capturing large commissions instead of offering advice. These are the people that have a solution or product ready for you before they even ask what your situation is, and it could mean that objectivity went out the window before they even met you!

So, **when looking for an objective financial advisor, *start* by looking for someone that is not an employee of a brokerage firm or bank.** This, of course, will not ensure that you will find a good and/or competent advisor, but at least you're not starting with someone who is mired in systemic conflicts of interest. Next, **make sure that a potential advisor not only has a good number of years of experience, but credentials that actually convey competence as well**.

Last, but certainly not least, **ask a lot of questions,** including: What experience do you have? How many clients do you work with? What credentials do you have, and what do they mean? How do you get paid? Are you offered more compensation for selling one product over another?

These questions are important because you need to…

Chapter 3

Avoid Conflicts of Interest Like the Plague

"I must create a system, or be enslaved by another man's."
– William Blake

A conflict of interest exists when your best interests do not align with the interests of the person giving you advice. When a conflict exists, it can cost you money. Unfortunately, the financial industry is riddled with conflicts of interest. Let me illustrate a few…

Let's start with the wirehouse brokerage firms, where I believe that entire system is basically built upon conflicts of interest. The whole premise of some brokerage and/or banks may be first and foremost to make money; giving advice to individuals just happens to be the secondary way they feed this monkey.

For reference, remember there were more of these firms a few years back, but they have been intricately involved in almost every financial crisis, such as the Tech Crash of 2000 and the Great Recession of 2008, and have voluntarily or involuntarily merged to avoid the junkyard.

These firms have built-in conflicts of interest based on their structure, what I like to call the "add-no-value layers of management." The first layer typically begins with a branch manager, although this person is generally just a sales manager for the firm.

Sure, branch managers have some oversight duties, but one of their responsibilities may also be to grow their branches' revenue (i.e., make more money for their firm). To do so, they might poke and prod advisors in their branch to work harder or maybe sell a higher commission product or program.

Some of these branch managers may also spend a lot of time (and money) trying to recruit new advisors from other firms, sometimes using large upfront bonuses to entice these other advisors to their firm. But the question that is begged is, "how does this benefit current clients like you?" In my opinion, these recruiting efforts don't help anyone other than the firm itself.

An additional job of this type of manager may be to organize sales events, which means bringing in so-called experts that want to tout their product or strategy to the branch's advisors. So, for instance, the manager may require all the advisors to attend a sales meeting put on by a specific fund company's wholesaler. But here's the rub: what do "sales" have to do with the advice business? Nothing at all!

Unfortunately, it doesn't end there. You see, most branch managers have regional managers that they answer to, and most regional managers answer to a national manager, and so on and so forth. And remember, all these different managers, who might be working to expand the firm's business rather than directly help the firm's clients, need to be paid, potentially adding a layer of costs to the firm that does not necessarily benefit the firm's clients.

Another huge conflict comes from proprietary products. These products are basically massive money-making conflicts of interest! Because if your advisor sells you a proprietary product, how do you know if it's the right product for you or just the right product for them to sell? It's simple; you don't! Even if it is the right product for you, how can you ever be 100% that the proprietary product was sold with good intentions? Again, you can't.

Long story made short, if you seek the help of an advisor, find one that is not encumbered by systemic conflicts of interests prevalent within the wirehouse brokerage firms and banks; search for an advisor who is not an employee of a bank, brokerage firm, or insurance company.

And regardless of whether you use an advisor or not, remember to always start with…

Chapter 4

The Basics: Stocks, Bonds and Cash

*"You must always start with something;
afterward you can remove all traces of reality."*
— Pablo Picasso

Stocks, bonds and cash – the three basic asset classes that almost every portfolio should hold. When thinking of each asset class, it's helpful to think of three different time buckets: short-term, mid-term, and long-term.

The short-term bucket is where you put cash or cash equivalents (checking, savings, etc). This bucket is meant to take care of your income needs over the next six to twelve months. What we don't want to do during this time frame is worry at all about the stock or bond markets.

The mid-term bucket is meant to be used after the short-term bucket, essentially for years two through ten (or fifteen or twenty, depending on your risk tolerance). Accordingly, your mid-term bucket should hold bonds, which are primarily for just two things: income and capital preservation. The income and historically low volatility of bonds during this time period let you ignore the volatility of the stock market, and give you the ability to allow stocks the time they need to potentially achieve their higher historical average annual return.

But don't forget that bonds can go up and down in value as well; they basically move inversely according to interest rates. When interest rates go down, bond values go up, and vice versa.

Here's a simple example: Let's say you buy a new five-year bond for $1000, and it pays 5% interest for five years. But after one year, you want to sell your bond. However, rates have gone up in the meantime, and now someone can buy a new five-year bond for $1000 that pays 6%. So, why would anyone pay you $1000 for your bond that only pays 5%? The answer is that they would not; a buyer will offer you something less than $1000, maybe $950 or so since your old bond only pays 5% versus a new bond that pays 6%.

The last bucket, the long-term one, is where you hold your stocks. This bucket is meant to be used after the short- and mid-term buckets. This is because if you can allow stocks ten or fifteen years of holding time, then they normally outperform bonds and cash. [1]

In fact, not only have stocks had an average annual return of 10% from 1926 through 2017 (versus 6% for bonds and 3% for cash)

---

[1]   Naturally, you will need to rebalance the buckets periodically, depending on your personal situation and market conditions. You may wish/need to have part of the mid-term bucket roll down to the short-term bucket. Further, depending on your risk tolerance, you may want to hold stocks for at least 15 years (or even twenty) instead of ten - meaning your mid-term bucket will now hold enough money in bonds to take care of years 2-15.

but stocks have outperformed bonds and cash over any ten- year time period 77 percent of the time, and 82 percent of the time over any fifteen-year time period. [2]

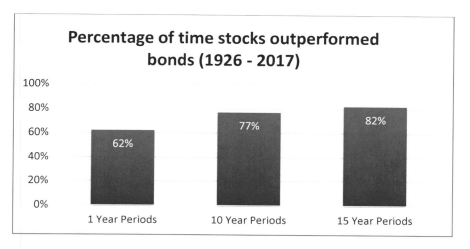

If you have the time (and patience), then you can potentially earn a higher long-term average annual return with stocks (remember, however, an average annual return is rarely earned in any one particular year). But if you don't have the time, then you shouldn't own stocks – it's that simple.

---

2   Source: Morningstar. Stocks represented by the Standard & Poor's 500 Stock Composite Index (S&P 500) 1957-2017, and the S&P 90 1926-1956; bonds represented by the Citigroup long-term, high-grade corporate bond total return index; cash represented by U.S. Treasury Bills, measured by rolling over each month a one-bill portfolio containing, at the beginning of each month, the bill having the shortest maturity not less than one month. The Standard & Poor's 500 Index is a capitalization weighted index of 500 stocks designed to measure performance of the broad domestic economy through changes in the aggregate market value of 500 stocks representing all major industries. Government bonds and Treasury bills are guaranteed by the US government as to the timely payment of principal and interest and, if held to maturity, offer a fixed rate of return and fixed principal value. Past performance is no guarantee of future results. An index is not managed and you cannot invest directly in an index. All return results assume monthly reinvestment of dividend or interest income. Yield and market value of bonds will fluctuate prior to maturity. The principal value of an investment in stocks fluctuates with changes in market conditions. These charts are for illustrative purposes only. Figures do not reflect the effects of taxes or transaction costs which would have a negative impact on investment results.

As a hypothetical, let's say you have $1 million, need $50,000 per year for expenses, and can give stocks a minimum of ten years. Then you could, to start, put $50,000 cash in your short-term bucket for year one. Assuming a 0% yield on your bonds for simplicity's sake, you could put $450,000 of bonds (nine years times $50,000) into your mid-term bucket for years two through ten. The remaining $500,000 can then go into stocks for ten years and beyond.

Unfortunately, when people allocate their portfolio to stocks, bonds or cash, they do not stop and contemplate what they are really trying to do. The cynic in me thinks that most people buy stocks or bonds based on their current level of fear or greed. But **the decision of the balance between stocks, bonds, and cash is one of the most, if not _the_ most important portfolio decision you can make.** Because it forms the basis of…

Chapter 5

Asset Allocation

"If a person knows not what harbor they seek,
any wind is the right wind."
– Seneca

In 1999, I held a workshop for about forty pre-retirees. I remember it well for two reasons. First, it was during the go-go days of the stock market; back then you could buy just about any stock, close your eyes, and make money – it was almost that easy. The second reason the workshop is so memorable is because of what happened afterwards.

We had just finished telling these pre-retirees that it makes sense for them to own bonds as well as stock so their conservative assets (bonds) could help balance the volatility of their riskier assets (stocks). Interestingly though, an older man came up to me and said, "You young punks don't know what you're talking about.

Stocks always have and always will make more sense for everyone's portfolio, whether you are young or old. Bonds are for losers!"

Well, I tried my best, but he was in no mood to hear that every portfolio, especially a retiree's, needed different asset classes to balance each other. Because **asset allocation is not only the first step when creating an investment portfolio, but it is the most important step as well**.

The theory behind asset allocation strategy was developed by Dr. Harry Markowitz. In 1952, he discovered that overall portfolio risk could be diminished by combining various asset classes whose returns were not perfectly correlated (i.e., some would zig when others zag, the basis of diversification).

This theory became known as modern portfolio theory (MPT), for which Markowitz received a Nobel Prize. What was revolutionary about Markowitz's theory was that he found that by combining different asset classes an investor could actually reduce the volatility of a portfolio while potentially increasing the return.

In furtherance of Markowitz's theory, Gary P. Brinson, Randolph L. Hood, and Gilbert L. Beebower studied the effects of asset allocation, where a diverse mix of non-correlated assets were combined, and verified its tremendous value to portfolio management. In fact, they proved that asset allocation is responsible for over ninety percent (90%) of a portfolio's return variability![3]

---

3   Source: Study by Gary Brinson, Brian Singer, and Gilbert Beebower, "Determinants of Portfolio Performance II," *Financial Analysts Journal*, January/February, 1995. The study analyzed data from 91 large corporate pension plans with assets of at least $100 Million over a 10-year period beginning in 1974.

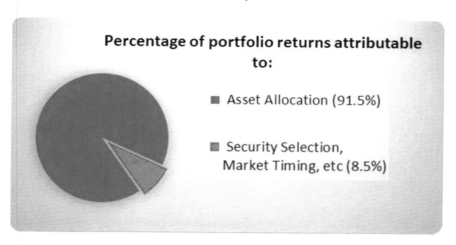

Percentage of portfolio returns attributable to:

■ Asset Allocation (91.5%)

■ Security Selection, Market Timing, etc (8.5%)

Did you catch that?! In essence, they proved that it is much more important to figure out what blend of asset classes will be in your portfolio than worry about when to buy or sell a security, much less what stock or bond to own.

In its simplest form, this means that your blend of stocks to bonds to cash is really the most important investment decision you can make. Sure, you can take it a step further and allocate to subclasses like large-cap (capitalization) domestic growth stocks, small-cap international value stocks, high-yield domestic bonds, domestic corporate bonds, etc, etc. But either way, the blend of the different asset classes will determine what happens over the long term.

Unfortunately, asset allocation is too often ignored or corrupted. It's ignored many times because people do not realize or respect the role that asset allocation plays within their portfolio's long-term performance; the corruption of asset allocation, however, is tougher to detect.

You see, true to form, Wall Street (in my opinion) took Brinson's research and turned it into another product: computer-generated "asset allocation" programs, usually in the form of five or six models that are created as a turnkey solution meant to work for anyone and everyone.

But these computer programs only work on numbers and not on people's actual situation, so the limited number of asset allocation models meant for anyone and everyone is just that: limiting. And when I say everyone, I mean everyone. Which is why, most times it seems, when you visit a large investment firm, it really may not matter which advisor you talk to, they are all going to offer you one of the same five or six pre-made blue suits (i.e., five or six asset allocation models) that everyone else gets, even if you want or need a different color suit.

And this is only the beginning. **The real harm is caused when an asset allocation plan is implemented without regard to other important variables,** such as cost or taxes.

For example, let's assume an investor has two different accounts, one is an IRA and the other is a non-IRA account. Since the two accounts have different tax treatments (an IRA is tax-deferred, the other is not), I would find it a bit too ironic if both accounts have the exact same securities with the exact same allocations.

In fact, I would be suspect of whatever advisor put together a portfolio like this. So I might ask two very simple questions: One, why do the IRA and non-IRA accounts have the exact same securities in the exact same percentages when the accounts have different tax treatments? And two, assuming this other advisor used a computer program to allocate and invest the client's money, what else does this "advisor" do for the investor to earn his/her fee?

Although I may be a cynic, I put quotes on "advisor" because sometimes I truly have no idea why someone is called an advisor when it seems they do not provide much advice. Instead, I fear some advisors are simply salespeople that just pride themselves on being asset gatherers, and their product of choice might just be a computer-generated asset allocation plan that uses high cost products.

So, remember that asset allocation, as important as it is, is not the end to all ends.[4] It is simply a means to an end; it is a means by which you begin to allocate your portfolio. But if you are not diligent and careful about the implementation of the allocation, you can end up...

---

4   Asset Allocation does not ensure a profit or protect against a loss. There is no guarantee that a diversified portfolio will enhance overall returns or outperform a non-diversified portfolio. Diversification dos not protect against market risk.

Chapter 6

Paying to be a Loser

"Never confuse movement with action."
– Ernest Hemingway

As important as asset allocation is to your success, you also need to understand that it is only a means to an end. Thus, the implementation of an asset allocation plan is extremely important as well.

There are basically two paths to take when implementing an asset allocation plan: you can use actively managed securities or passively managed securities. If you implement your portfolio with actively managed securities, then you or someone else is going to pick stocks and bonds to try and beat some relative benchmark for each part of your portfolio.

With passive securities, you are only looking to match the benchmark for each part of your portfolio; thus, a passive fund will simply try to own the same securities as the benchmark it is trying to follow and/or replicate.

For instance, if you decide to place twenty percent of your portfolio in large-cap growth stocks, then with active securities you or someone else (such as a financial advisor or mutual fund manager) will actively trade those types of stocks hoping to beat the Russell 1000 Growth Index (or some other relevant benchmark).[5] If you use passive securities, then you would use a fund or security that simply owns the stocks that the Russell 1000 Growth Index holds – no more, no less.

Now, before you make your choice as to how to implement your asset allocation, with active or passive securities, let's introduce a little common sense and logic.

First, if you are going to try to pick individual stocks and bonds (active security selection), then you have to start with the assumption that, all things being equal, someone who has more time and resources to research stocks and bonds is going to be better at picking stocks and bonds.

As an individual investor, it can be very hard to match the resources that a professional manager has; this can hold true for advisors as well, since they hopefully spend some time advising clients. Accordingly, all things being equal, we believe a fund manager should be better than you or an advisor at actively picking stocks and bonds.

---

5   The Russell 1000 Index consists of 1,000 largest securities in the Russell 3000 Index, which represents approximately 90% of the total market capitalization of the Russell 3000 Index. It is a large-cap, market-oriented index and is highly correlated with the S&P 500 Index. This is an unmanaged index which cannot be invested into directly.

So, through simple logic, we have narrowed down our choice to either having a fund manager actively trading large-cap growth stocks (*hoping* to beat the Russell 1000 Growth Index for that twenty percent of your portfolio), or simply trying to track the Russell 1000 Growth Index using a passive security.

Second, we need to remind ourselves that the most important decision, asset allocation, the one that determines ninety percent of your portfolio's direction (please refer to Chpt 5, Asset Allocation), has already been made, so now we are only talking about the other ten percent.

Third, if you choose active securities, you will pay significantly more than those who use passive securities. The average annual expense ratio for an actively managed U.S. large-cap equity mutual fund is 0.72%, whereas the average annual expense ratio for a passively managed U.S. equity index fund is just 0.09%.[6]

Fourth, research indicates that over certain periods of time the majority of actively managed funds tend to underperform their benchmark; just look at the results over a fifteen-year time period ending December 31, 2017 (see chart on next page).

This table may indicate that the small number of managers able to outperform their benchmark in some asset classes may not be any greater than what someone might expect by chance; in other words, the ones that actually beat their benchmark may only be lucky.

And fifth, to top it off, not only are the odds against you picking a good manager since few of them beat their benchmark consistently, but you need to pick that manager *before* the results are in!

---

6   Sources: Vanguard, using data from Lipper, a Thomson Reuters Company, as of December 31, 2017.

So even if you choose one of the few active managers who beat their benchmark in the past, you have no idea if they will do so again in the future!

The investment community's clear understanding that the future is absolutely unpredictable is exactly why the most pervasive, yet sadly most disregarded disclaimer, is "past performance is no guarantee of future results."

In other words, just because someone picked the right stocks or bonds yesterday, does not mean they will pick the right stocks and bonds tomorrow. The future is unpredictable, and trying to pick the winners ahead of time is a crapshoot at best. But with your investment portfolio, it's an expensive crapshoot.

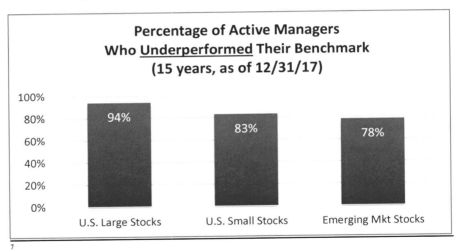

7

---

7   These percentages have been adjusted for survivorship bias, whereby the results of existing funds in an analysis may be bolstered by the merging or discontinuation of underperforming funds. Performance data reflect 15 years through December 31, 2017. Sources: Vanguard calculations, using data from Morningstar, Inc., MSCI, Standard & Poor's, and Barclays Capital. U.S. large stocks are represented by large blend (MSCI US Prime Market 750 Index through 01/30/2013, CRSP US Large Cap Index thereafter); U.S. small stocks are represented by small blend (Russell 2000 Index through 05/16/2003, MSCI US Small Cap 1750 Index through 01/30/2013, CRSP US Small Cap Index.

OK, I know what some people are going to say… "But Tim, the graph above only represents one-time period." (In this case, a fifteen-year track record ending in 2017). Well fine, I encourage you to look into this further on your own. Because if you do, you will reach the same conclusion: that stock and bond pickers are just not that good at picking stocks and bonds.

So, what do you do? It's simple: remember that **securities, or any product for that matter, are nothing more than implementation tools. They only help you implement a previously determined asset allocation plan.** Just use the most efficient tools available, which are passive securities in most cases, to implement your asset allocation plan. Don't pay to be a loser by overpaying for active securities that typically underperform.

By taking this approach, you will naturally focus on what's important (the allocation plan) rather than the implementation tools, and you will probably outperform the majority of actively managed funds simply by controlling the controllable variables. Which is why I continually tell people to…

---

thereafter); emerging market stocks are represented by the MSCI Emerging Markets Index. You cannot invest in an index. Past performance is no guarantee of future results. The prices of small cap stocks prices of small cap stocks are generally more volatile than large cap stocks. International investing involves special risks such as currency fluctuation and political instability and may not be suitable for all investors. These risks are often heightened for investments in emerging markets. Asset allocation does not ensure a profit or protect against a loss.

Chapter 7

Control What You Can Control

"You can't always control the wind,
but you can control the sails."
— Anthony Robbins

I have learned that **there are some things in life that you cannot control. The attempt to do so is not only pointless but can be a waste of your time, money, and patience**. In fact, one of my favorite quotes is the Serenity Prayer: "God, grant me the serenity to accept the things I cannot change, courage to change the things I can, and the wisdom to know the difference." If you get nothing else out of this book, I promise this quote will help you in all facets of your life.

In trying to discern what things are uncontrollable (i.e., things we cannot change or that are unchangeable, if that's really a word), and thus accept rather than fret about them, it's good to start with things that are unpredictable, such as future events.

Since future events are, by definition, in the future and therefore unknowable and unpredictable, they are also uncontrollable. Sure, we can make guesses based on current and historical references as to what might happen in the future, but the simple fact remains that the future is unpredictable with one hundred percent accuracy and is therefore uncontrollable.

The weather is a great analogy. I think everyone has to agree that most weather forecasters, if you go out beyond a few days, are just not that good; no fault of their own, it's just that a forecast of the weather is unpredictable since it's in the future.

Yes, they can make an educated guess from current and historical weather patterns, but Mother Nature will get the final say, and an educated guess is ultimately just that – a guess. And if we guess today that it will rain a week from today, we must admit two things: one, that we are really just guessing, and two, that if it actually rains a week from today, then we will have been more lucky than smart with our prediction.

The stock and bond markets are the same as the weather. We have no way of knowing what the markets will do in the future; we can only make educated guesses as to which direction the markets will go in the future – because it's in the future!

Again, we can look to historical references, but we need to always remember that past performance is absolutely no indication of future results. So, similar to the weather, **since the markets are unpredictable and uncontrollable, why try to control them when it can't be done? It's dumb to even try**.

Instead, take control of what you can control. And while you are doing this, remember that portfolio management does not a financial plan make, meaning that your overall financial situation is much more than just your investment portfolio. So, not only should you control the controllable variables within your portfolio as we discussed previously, but you should also seek to control variables within your overall financial plan.

Tax allocation, whereby you hold certain asset classes of your portfolio in one type of account versus another, may be one controllable variable that could make a difference in time.

Let's say, for instance, that you have money in a tax-deferred IRA as well as in a regular taxable account. **As always, much depends on your particular situation, but it might make sense to hold your stock in the non-IRA account and bonds in the IRA.** This lets you keep the interest from the bonds tax-deferred in your IRA. Holding stocks in your non-IRA account may help you utilize the historically lower capital gains tax rates when you sell.

And don't forget, a stock's growth is also inherently tax-deferred since the capital gains tax isn't applied until after you sell the stock. And if you have any realized losses on your stocks in the non-IRA account, you can use them to offset gains as well as $3,000 of income per year. As a final legacy, your heirs may utilize a stepped-up cost basis on stock once you pass away. (Please remember that tax laws always change, and you need to consult your tax professional.)

Unfortunately, most people think that taking control of their taxes means just searching for more deductions to lower their current tax bill. But this approach is essentially retroactive reporting for past or current taxes, rather than proactive planning against *future* tax obligations, which is actually a very controllable variable.

Speaking of controllable variables, I would be remiss if I didn't quickly discuss the philosophical aspect of taking control. In fact, I truly believe that the main reason sometimes people do not take control of certain aspects of their lives (controlling the controllable variables) is because taking control means making a change, and I believe many people fear change, even if it is good for them. Think about it, how many times have you held off on making a change in your life even though you knew the end result should/would ultimately be better? Maybe just as the only thing to fear in life is fear itself, so too may it be that change itself is the scariest part of changing direction for the better (Ok, so much for the amateur philosophy!).

As for other controllable variables in finances, they include, among others, asset allocation, security implementation, IRA distributions, Roth conversions, mortgage decisions, social security planning, business financing, retirement plan contributions, education planning, etc, etc.

And let's not forget the most controllable variable of all: spending. In fact, I'm convinced that if people spent as much time on creating and sticking to a reasonable budget as they do watching the stock market, there would be far fewer people in foreclosure every year.

So next time you order that ever-fattening double-mocha, half-caff, extra-smooth frappuccino that costs more than your lunch, stop and remember the variables that you can control! And while you're watching your budget...

Chapter 8

Do Not Overpay for Advice or Product

"There was a time when a fool and his money were soon parted, but now it happens to everybody."
– Adlai E. Stevenson

One simple thing people can control is fees. But amazingly, many people just don't seem to care, which is lazy and dumb. Sorry, no offense intended, but "stupid is as stupid does", as Forrest Gump taught us.

John Bogle, founder of Vanguard Funds, verbalized my thoughts perfectly when he said, "asset allocation is critically important, but **cost is also critically important**. When compared to these two issues, all the other factors that go into investing in a diversified portfolio of high-grade stocks and bonds pale into insignificance."

There are two basic costs involved with investing: advisory and product. Advisory costs, although I admittedly have a bias, are the more important of the two. Advisors can act as essential coordinators of your comprehensive plan, not only offering comprehensive, objective advice, but also helping with investment management, as well as tax, insurance, and estate planning strategies. They can help manage all those controllable variables that I listed in the previous chapter, and they should certainly try to contain the internal portfolio fees I discussed in chapter six.

Further, an advisor may have the ability to help control the potential failure associated with self-management. Witness the findings of the 2018 Dalbar Associates study, "Quantitative Analysis of Investor Behavior" (1996-2017). In the study, the S&P 500 index had an average annualized return of 7.2% over that twenty year period, yet the average equity fund investor had only gained 5.29% during the same time frame. The explanation for the discrepancy is emotionally-induced changes within an investor's portfolio, and cost.

So I will again reiterate the fact that I believe everyone can benefit from an objective financial advisor. However, I also strongly feel that too many advisors, good and bad, charge too much for their services. What's reasonable in my eyes, you ask? Well, the lower the better, but one percent seems fair; anything above one hundred and twenty-five basis points (1.25%) is simply dumb to pay because it's prohibitively expensive. It creates too high a "fee hurdle" for your assets to overcome, and the advice simply may not be worth the fee.

When it comes to paying an advisor - if that's the route you take - the other two pieces of advice are this: One, only pay for *comprehensive* financial advice, not just for asset management.

A true financial advisor should proactively help with any issue that affects your finances, from buying a car to planning for retirement, and everything in between. And two, make sure the fee goes down as the assets go up. If the advisor charges one percent of assets on a $1 million portfolio (again, for comprehensive advice not just asset management), then the fee should be closer to 70 basis points (0.7%) or less if the assets under management are $2 million, and that fee should continue to go down as the assets go up.

Now, before I move onto product cost, which is where I think most people get hosed (as my son would say), I want to discuss commissions quickly. If you noticed, I have pretty much skipped them so far; let me tell you why.

First, if you are a do-it-yourselfer, then just find a firm that offers the lowest commission. Again, this is one of those things that you can control, and the cheaper it is the better if you don't want anything other than trade execution. Second, if you are working with an advisor, then it may not make sense to pay commissions.

The reason is simple: when you are paying a commission for the purchase or sale of a security, you simply may not know if the buy or sell recommendations from the advisor are made for your best interest or in order to generate that commission. So, assuming trust is essential when using an advisor, and except in certain situations, **commissions can be a massive conflict of interest that could make full trust impossible.**

As for product cost, this is where most people seem to be asleep at the wheel. This is one of the variables people can control, yet most tend not to! They forget that the only thing they should be paying for is objective advice, not for uncontrollable returns (see chapter six, Paying to be a Loser).

Long story made short: **do not pay too much for advice or product, and control the controllable**, which can also be done through…

Chapter 9

Market Timing vs. Time in the Market

"An economist is an expert who will know tomorrow why the things he predicted yesterday didn't happen today."
– Laurence J. Peter

Do you remember when the economic powers-that-be declared at the end of 2008 that a recession had started in December of 2007? How smart they were to be able to tell us, after the fact, what we already knew! If only it were so easy to decide when to buy or sell a security!

The fact of the matter is that predicting the future is impossible. Unfortunately, we human beings far too often equate luck with skill.

For example: Let's say I stand on the side of the road and declare that the next car to pass will be red. If the first car that passes is blue, you'll probably laugh that I got it wrong. If I correctly guess the color of the next car that passes, you'll likely think I got lucky.

But, if I correctly guess the color of the third car to pass, you might think I know something. Worse still, after I correctly guess the color of the fourth and fifth car, you'll probably think I have some sort of gift and ask me what the next lotto number will be! My lucky guesses could make you think I have some sort of skill that I really don't possess!

The holds true with getting in and out of the market (buying and selling, respectively), also known as "timing the market." Most people, investors and advisors alike, think that if they sell right before the market falls, then they have some sort of gift to know when to get out; that false sense of confidence gets reinforced if they buy right before the market goes up. But they fail to realize that they may have only gotten lucky, because no one knows for sure what is going to happen tomorrow – it's simply impossible!

This is why some of the best stock pickers, including Warren Buffett, remind everyone that they may be nothing more than lucky, and that **most people are better off not only avoiding stock selection, but also not trying to guess the best time to buy or sell stocks.** Instead, what matters is how long you are in the market, thus the phrase that "it's not timing the market, but time in the market." Because though you may get lucky, you may get unlucky too and end up buying high and selling low instead.

And if you get unlucky just a few times, and miss just a few of the best days over a period of time, it can negatively affect your returns. Just take a look at what a mistake it would have been in the past to time the stock market and miss some of the best days from 1996 through 2017.

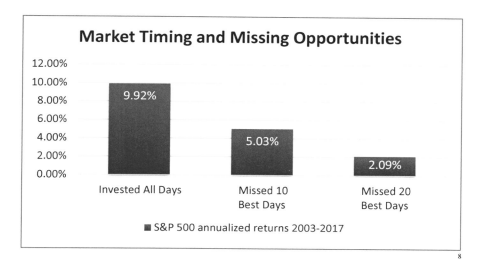

Market Timing and Missing Opportunities

S&P 500 annualized returns 2003-2017

- Invested All Days: 9.92%
- Missed 10 Best Days: 5.03%
- Missed 20 Best Days: 2.09%

So, if you are going to buy a security, then just do it and stop thinking about it. Sure, if you're putting a portfolio together, you can dollar cost average over a six- or twelve-month time period (which is what you are doing by automatically contributing to a 401(k) or some similar plan). But otherwise remember that trying to correctly time the market is a waste of time [9]

This is also why I tell investors that the first page of their monthly statement is pretty meaningless. Seriously, the first page, which tells you what the portfolio's value is at the end of the month, is really irrelevant. First, by the time you receive your statement in the mail, the account value is outdated; the markets will have changed by the

---

[8]   Source: Standard & Poor's. The chart above illustrates that missing the most significant rising market days has historically reduced returns. This chart is for illustrative purposes only, and is not indicative of the performance of any specific investment. This hypothetical illustration is based on the Standard & Poor's 500 Composite Index with dividends reinvested over the 20 year period of 1996 to 2017. Past performance is no guarantee of future results; an index is unmanaged and is unavailable for direct investment.

[9]   Dollar cost averaging involves continuous investment in securities regardless of fluctuation in price levels of such securities. An investor should consider their ability to continue purchasing through fluctuating price levels. Such a plan does not assure a profit and does not protect against loss in declining markets.

time the statement is printed. Second, the value is only telling you what you would get if you sold everything at that specific point in time, which you did not do, and would not do.

Don't get me wrong, I am not telling you to never sell stocks. You should sell when your holding period (say, ten years) is near, at hand, or in the past. You should also periodically adjust your stock holdings based on your asset allocation plan. **But don't go buying and/or selling stocks just because you "think" the market is going up or down next week – because you don't know what is going to happen in the future!**

So, be careful of the people, especially some of the talking-heads on television, who either purposefully or inadvertently make you think that they can predict the future. And also be aware of...

Chapter 10

The Games the Industry Plays

"The universe is full of wonderful things,
patiently waiting for our wits to grow sharper."
– Eden Phillpotts

Did you know that there are almost as many mutual funds as there are stocks in the United States? Do you know why that is? Because the more funds that the fund companies offer the better the chance you will invest in one of them. And the more money people put into the funds, the more money the funds make.

Don't kid yourself that all the funds are there to help you be a better investor. That might be one of their goals, but the primary goal is to make money for the fund company. Heck, if the fund industry wanted to help you, they would probably shut down a bunch of funds considering that the majority of them consistently underperform the benchmark they are trying to beat.

Instead, the fund industry likes to play games. Like what, you ask? Well, let's start with "survivorship bias". Remember in chapter six, where I told you that the majority of funds underperformed the benchmark they were trying to beat? Well, many times the numbers do not account for the funds that did not survive the testing period, helping make the remaining funds' performance look better than reality.

You see, survivorship bias can distort the results of a timed analysis. For instance, let's assume you have ten runners who are going to run a one-mile race, and we want to know how many finish within five minutes. During the race, two runners drop out due to exhaustion and do not finish the race. So, only eight runners finish the race, four of which run the mile under five minutes. Without adjusting for survivorship bias, we would say that 50% of the runners (4 of 8) finished the race under five minutes. However, if we include the two runners that dropped out of the race (i.e., we adjust for survivorship bias), then only 40% of the runners (4 out of the original 10) finished under five minutes.

So, results can look better if you do not adjust for survivorship bias. And we believe the same thing happens in the mutual fund industry; some funds just do not survive long enough to have, say, a 10 or 15-year track record. What's happened? Well, they may have died a quiet death, one the fund industry probably hopes you didn't take note of. You see funds that perform badly may get shut down or merged into other funds, leaving fewer funds to compare to the benchmark. Thus, **"survivorship bias" makes the funds' results look better than they otherwise would**.

Just think about it: if, during a certain time period, 1,000 out of the *surviving* 4,500 funds outperformed their benchmark, then that's about twenty-two percent (22%) that did well (which seems, pretty crappy – and yes, that's a technical term). But if 1,000 out of the original 5,000 funds outperformed, then only twenty percent (20%) outperformed (even crappier!). And if you don't believe this happens, just look to the research. For instance, a Dimensional Fund Advisor study ("The US Mutual Fund Landscape, 2018") found there were 2,867 US-domiciled equity funds and 1,452 bond funds at the start of a five-year period beginning in January of 2013. However, by the end of that five-year period, only 82% of the equity funds and 86% of the bonds funds were still around; the other 18% and 14%, respectively, simply did not even survive that five-year period!

And remember, just because a fund did well over the last three or five years, or even the last ten years, this does not mean it will do well over the coming years. Unfortunately, far too many people do what I call **"track-record investing." Based on historical performance, they buy a security or fund that did well yesterday hoping/thinking it will do well tomorrow, ignoring the fact that it may not do well in the future because the future is unknowable and thus unpredictable!**

The better way to invest is to create an asset allocation plan that makes sense for your specific situation and timeline. Then implement that plan with the most cost-efficient securities and ignore the noise!

Ignore the one-, three-, or five-year returns being touted by the fund companies. Ignore the magazine ads that show a beautiful couple relaxing on the beach because they invested in ABC funds. Ignore the commercials that make you think all you need to do is use XYZ funds to become wealthy.

My favorite commercial to hate, laugh at, or better yet, ignore, was a mutual fund company commercial from the late 1990s. Their message was to make sure you "don't miss the boat," intimating that you needed to get in (their funds) while the gettin' was good.[10]

What a joke! There is never any boat to be missed! And wow, what horrible timing that would have been in any event since it was right before the tech crash of 2000!

While we're on the topic of noise and things to ignore, let me remind you that…

---

10   Investing in mutual funds involves risk, including possible loss of principal. No strategy assures success or protects against loss.

Chapter 11

The Media is not Your Friend

"Television has raised writing to a new low."
— Samuel Goldwyn

Someone once asked me why the stock market was so volatile - why it went up for no apparent reason, only to go down the next day for some other reason. To me, it makes complete sense. At the end of the day, the market is just a bunch of human beings trading stocks and bonds - and we human beings are nothing if not emotional, and tend to act erratically and volatile at times due to our emotions.

With investments, our emotions really get narrowed down to just two: fear and greed. So the media, especially the television media, does two things. First, they play on our emotions of fear and greed. Second, they generate a lot of noise to try and keep our attention, which then helps them to sell the advertisements.

Playing upon our emotions is actually pretty simple. Remember, all the media needs to do is either make you think you will lose money (fear) or miss out on some great opportunity (greed) if you do not pay attention.

But how do they keep your attention? That's simple too: they just create a false sense of alarm, so that you feel like you *need* to pay attention. Then they put on the show, or the circus as I like to call it.

How else can you explain why we have "breaking news" just about every day on almost every TV channel? Seriously, when was the last time you watched some breaking news and thought, "Wow, that's a life changer – I'm glad I got that news right away?!" My guess is you forgot all about whatever breaking news it was five minutes after it broke.

And if you think that my calling the financial media a circus is too strong a word, then explain the clowns to me. Tell me why there is a talking head on TV who literally yells, whoops and presses stupid noise buttons while talking about something as mundane as the balance sheet of a company! It defies logic, other than to realize that a lot (not all) of financial media is entertainment - no more, no less.

This is exactly why I say you should **ignore the noise that comes out of the media, since it has very little relevance!**

Sure, there might be a little bit of substance (emphasis on "little"), and they may help by offering some tidbits of useful information (emphasis on "tidbits"). But at the end of the day, their job is to entertain you. They do this by appealing to your fear and greed, not your understanding or intellect, and hope that by sensationalizing the non-sensational you will continue to watch the media circus.

And this is where it gets interesting. Because now we need to figure out who the clowns actually work for. If you say the television outlets or stations, the ones that produce the circus, then you are only partially correct. In fact, the media must answer to the companies that pay their bills, the companies that pay for the commercials.

Think about it! Is the stock market news reporter looking wild-eyed and exasperated when the Dow Jones is down one hundred points because she's worried about your finances? Or is she instead taking a ho-hum day, where one hundred points up or down in one day means nothing over a ten-year time frame, and making it seem like the world's shaking in its boots so you'll tune in more?

The answer is easy; they want you to tune into the show and watch the circus, as well as the commercials that pay their bills. And which industry has the most companies that pay for these commercials, and thus sponsor the circus? You guessed it, the financial industry. Go figure!

It may not be a conflict of interest, but unfortunately too many people rely upon the information being pushed by the media, which is in turn being fed or sponsored by financial firms that are built, first and foremost, to make money off of you.

My hope is that more people will become aware of what is happening to them, or more appropriately, what they are doing to themselves by paying too much attention or giving too much credit to the noise generated by the media.

Viewers of media need to be aware of the hidden agendas; similarly, "buyer beware" should be the name of the game for consumers looking to buy certain services or products, especially since...

Chapter 12

Every Product Can Be a Good Product or a Bad Product

"There are worse things than death.
Have you ever spent an evening
with an insurance salesman?"
– Woody Allen

Remember when I said that asset allocation accounts for ninety percent of your portfolio's success and direction? Well, that has to mean that whatever else you do, whether it's market timing, security selection, or who knows what, it can only account for ten percent of your portfolio's success. As I said, after the asset allocation is determined, then you really just need to find the most efficient implementation tools.

When you start looking at the tools, however, there are products that are not necessarily securities, but rather strategies-in-a-box.

They come in lots of different flavors, and can be good or bad depending on the situation. I have seen a product used appropriately for one person, yet the same product completely misused in another person's situation. In other words: **what works well for one person does not necessarily work for another person**.

Since some of these products tend to be sold more often than bought, I will give you a quick overview of some of the most popular, starting with variable annuities.

In essence, variable annuities are tax-deferred insurance products that contain both an investment and insurance component. They not only offer a pre-set bunch of subaccounts (portfolios of securities that are similar to mutual funds), but also a living and/or death benefit "guarantee", which could account for why they may be common with an older crowd. The trick is figuring out what these "guarantees" actually offer, and how they work.

Typically, they work like this: Let's say you invest $100,000 in a variable annuity. You get to choose which of the subaccounts the money is invested in; the subaccounts will go up and down with the markets, but remain tax-deferred. Next, aside from the fluctuating account value of the subaccounts, you are given some sort of "guarantee."[11]

So, in this example, regardless of how the subaccounts perform, the insurance company might also guarantee a living benefit and death benefit that increases each year by, say, five percent. Thus, if the subaccount's value is worth only $60,000 ten years later due to

---

11   The investment returns and principal value of the available sub-account portfolios will fluctuate so that the value of an investor's unit, when redeemed, may be worth more or less than their original value.

poor market performance (and high fees), then the living and death benefit guarantee will still have grown to $150,000.

But there are some serious caveats. First, and most importantly, any "guarantee" is only as good as the claims paying ability of the insurance company that offers it. Second, in order to collect the death benefit you must die. Third, that living benefit normally does not guarantee a $150,000 lump sum. Instead, the $150,000 "benefit" typically only allows you to pull a certain percentage out each year (in the example above, you may only be allowed to withdraw four percent of the $150,000 living benefit per year). Last, but not least, you may be forced to stay in these products, or strategies-in-a-box, for a period of years if you do not want to pay a large surrender fee.

Don't forget that these so-called guarantees are sometimes marketed as something that can help you through tough market environments. But that could be hindsight, since, hopefully, some of the toughest times are behind us (anyone remember the Tech Crash of 2000 or the Great Recession of 2007-2010?); in a sense, it could be like getting car insurance *after* an accident.

Variable annuities are expensive too. When you add up the admin and sub-account fees, the mortality and expense risk charges, and contract fees, as well as the living or death benefit rider fees, you may be paying three to four percent in fees per year. And, oh by the way, the high fees also compensate the agent or "advisor" (sometimes quite generously, which is why they may be oversold).

Now, don't get me wrong, I like and use variable annuities in our practice – but *only if* they work for the specific situation. And if the situation does call for an annuity or any other product, we use them sparingly, remembering that you never put too much money in anything! Further, there are so many pros and cons to each strategy-in-a-box such as an annuity that the client needs to be well informed before buying one. For instance, it's important to note that variable annuities, like all annuities, have limitations with regard to withdrawals; withdrawals made prior to age 59½ are subject to a 10% IRS penalty tax and surrender charges may apply. Further, gains from tax-deferred investments are taxable as ordinary income upon withdrawal.

A close cousin to the variable annuity, and one that's pushed too often in my opinion, is an equity index annuity ("EIA"). This insurance product, although many times sold as if it were an investment product, is nothing more than a contract with an insurance company.

In contrast to a variable annuity, which has an investment component through the subaccounts, an EIA's value is completely reliant upon the issuing insurance contract. Through this contract with the insurance company, the premium paid is generally credited with an interest rate that is linked to an equity index such as the S&P 500. However, it's important to remember that there is no investment component, just the contract with the insurance company – which is why the only license someone needs to sell these things is an insurance license, which is a bit scary!

One of the scarier stories I've heard came from an air conditioner repairman I met about eight years ago; he had come to our house to fix our A/C unit. Knowing that I worked in finance, he asked if I had ever heard of an equity index annuity. I said "Yes, why do you ask?" He said, "Well, I just made eight thousand dollars by selling one of those things!"

So I asked, "You did what? I thought you were an A/C repairman?!" And he said, "It was easy. All I had to do was study for a month to take a state insurance exam and get my license. Then I found this old lady who had eighty thousand dollars to invest, so I sold her an equity index annuity and got paid eight thousand dollars in commission! Not bad for a day's work, huh?!"

Call me crazy, but this A/C repairman seemed much more interested in making a quick buck than helping this woman. In fact, this type of product has many features that should be disclosed to any potential buyer before it is bought. This should include a list of fees, surrender charges, liquidity options, and safeguards, among others. Further, the seller of these products should do a thorough analysis to see if the product, regardless of how good it may actually be, is even suitable for a specific potential buyer. But in this case, these concerns were not addressed.

Unfortunately, my guess is that this happens far too often. There are too many salespeople or so-called advisors taking what otherwise might be a decent product and selling it inappropriately. As I like to say, good dog, bad owner (i.e., the product may not be bad, just the salesperson who misuses or oversells it for their own benefit).

And I would be remiss if I did not mention the knucklehead salespeople who are not intentionally misusing a product, but misuse it anyhow due to a lack of care, training, or experience (sorry, ignorance is no defense with me). Some of these salespeople, who may call themselves "advisors," are looking to close a sale rather than give you objective advice.

Many of these salespeople put on seminars that might to be about financial planning, but usually end up promoting one product over another. That's why I tell everyone to be aware of these product-based sales pitches, because…

Chapter 13

A Free Lunch Seminar
May Cost You More Than a Meal

"There is no such thing as a free lunch."
– Milton Friedman

When I started in the business back in 1996, we held educational workshops every month or so. Our purpose was to simply inform people of basic financial concepts, as well as some things everyone should be aware of, like how to make sure you are not paying too much in fees - a lot of stuff that formed the basis for this book. After a year or so, two things happened.

First, many clients told us that they were starting to receive lots of invitations to other seminars. After encouraging our clients to attend those other seminars – figuring the more education someone gets, the better – they told us how different the other seminars were. They said that in contrast to our workshops, where they just got some good education, the other seminars seemed to push one product or another.

The second thing that happened was that we started receiving a lot of calls from wholesalers who wanted to "sponsor" our workshops. They said that if we allowed them to speak at our workshops, then they would pay for the cost of the workshop. Now, before I tell you why we would not allow a wholesaler to speak at our seminars, much less push any product, let me tell you what a wholesaler does.

A wholesaler is a person that tries to get advisors to sell certain products to their clients. But here's the catch: they only work for a single investment company. So the wholesaler may basically be a one-trick pony; they may only have one company's products to sell, regardless of how good or bad that company or its products may be.

For instance, a wholesaler from ABC Compnay (a hypothetical company) may try to convince me why ABC's products or investments are the greatest thing since sliced bread and that I should use them in all my client's portfolios. It really doesn't matter to the wholesaler who the end client is; in fact, they normally never even meet the client. Nevertheless, they will insist they have a product that is a solution for the client, and might even insist that the product is a solution for *every* client!

But in my mind, that doesn't make sense. If the wholesaler doesn't know the investor, how do they know if their product is good for a specific investor, much less any and all investors? To me, this is kind of like saying, "Hey, I don't know what the problem is, but I definitely have the solution." Crazy, huh?! But that's the way it works, unfortunately. Although I believe there are some very intelligent wholesalers that can offer some decent investment insight, the fact of the matter is that a wholesaler's job is not to help the client, but to simply have advisors sell their specific company's products.

So here's why we are skeptical of wholesalers, and why we think you need to be careful if you attend a luncheon or other event sponsored (i.e., paid for) a wholesaler: because if the wholesaler is paying for the event, then the advisor may feel like they owe the wholesaler some business – even if the wholesaler's product may not be right for a certain client. And please do not misunderstand me - I am not making a judgment on the product or the wholesaler, but rather that the trust between the client and advisor should be immune from any potential conflict of interest. Remember, the job of a truly objective advisor is to find the right product for a client's specific situation. It is not to have a pre-set selection of products to sell to a client regardless of their situation!

But as I said before, I worry there may be too many salespeople that call themselves advisors, and I also worry that a lot of these **free-lunch seminars may be nothing more than product pitches**. I worry that some of these so-called advisors are really just trying to entice you with a free meal so they can try to sell you a product, or the seminar is sponsored (i.e. paid for) by a wholesaler who will in turn expect the so-called advisor to sell their company's product for them.

And if you think this happens only to the less wealthy or unsophisticated, think again. The wealthy and sophisticated get the same push, just in a fancier setting. In fact…

Chapter 14

High Net Worth Clients Just Get More Crap

"Illusion is the first of all pleasures."
— Oscar Wilde

When I worked at a national wirehouse brokerage firm, before becoming an independent financial advisor, I went on a company trip to Florida. I called it an "incentive" trip since the firm offered to pay some or all of the trip expenses for certain advisors who generated enough money for the firm.

While on the trip, I spoke with an executive of the firm and asked him about the great new racing boat that the firm was "sponsoring" in global sporting events (remember, "sponsor" means pay for). Figuring that my clients had paid the firm a lot of money over the years and thus helped buy the boat, I asked, tongue in cheek, if my clients would ever be able to sail on the boat

Well, let's just say the question was not well received. However, after he walked away, his assistant made clear that if I had an extremely wealthy client then they might "see what they could do."

I remember the line because I thought "what a bunch of crap" for two reasons: one, why can't the firm's clients who helped pay for the boat sail on it, and two, do wealthy people really give a company their money simply because they get to ride on a nice boat? Unfortunately, the answer is quite often "yes."

You see, I know from working with people of all means that **most financial advice transcends wealth levels**. Sure, there are times when the wealthy need and have access to products or strategies that less wealthy people either do not need or do not have access to. But the majority of the time, the wealthy need the same types of advice or products, just in larger quantities. Too often the wealthy overpay for junk they don't need.

A good example of this is someone I know who lives in California and happens to use another advisor for his asset management. His investment portfolio is worth almost $20 million, and he thinks he's getting a good deal because he only pays forty basis points (.40%) on the asset management of his portfolio.

But I pointed out to him that it still costs him almost $80,000 per year! And why, if a $1 million portfolio managed at one percent costs $10,000 a year, should his portfolio cost eight times more? Sure, he might get a bit more attention from the advisor, but just because his allocation plan calls for a $2 million large-cap growth allocation instead of $200,000, does that extra attention warrant an additional $70,000 in fees? I think not!

However, my friend told me he is treated like royalty when he visits their beautifully decorated office. My only response was that for $80,000 a year he'd better be treated like royalty!

You see, I believe that a lot of wealthy investors may be paying too much for really nice smoke and mirrors, not to mention wood-paneled offices. In fact, it's possible that a lot of **wealthy people may incorrectly believe they are getting better advice and/or service simply because they are paying for a glitzier illusion.**

It's not dissimilar from how some people wouldn't be caught dead shopping for peanuts in Walmart, even though they are getting the exact same stuff at a higher price in a fancy grocery store. And if you think you are getting an upgraded product, be careful what you shop for. Again, similar to that fancy grocery store that sells the premium nuts you cannot find in Walmart, the premium nuts may not be all they're cracked up to be (all pun intended).

Take hedge funds for instance, the seemingly exclusive province of the wealthy, since you need to have a high net worth to even be eligible to buy such a product. These products offer the *potential ability* (just like any other fund, hedged or not) to outperform some market index, and tantalize the rich with returns you only read about in the newspapers.

However, Hedge Fund Research ("HFR") found that hedge funds tend to underperform the S&P 500. In fact, from 2006 through 2015, HFR found that the average hedge fund only gained about 3.4% annually whereas the S&P 500 annualized 7% (in 2017, hedge funds averaged 8.5% whereas the S&P 500 gained 21.8%). Defying logic, however, hedge fund assets increased during that same time frame! Proving Aristotle's point that "probable impossibilities are preferable to improbable possibilities."[12]

If this sounds familiar, read chapter six again ("Paying to be a Loser"), because the same thing holds true here: **it's nearly impossible to consistently beat the market, or whatever index you choose to challenge, and the actively managed funds (hedge or otherwise) that do outperform some index are more lucky than smart.**

That's why I think the only real accomplishment that hedge funds have consistently had is the money they've generated for themselves since they often charge high management fees of around 2% of assets under management plus 20% of any profits earned ("New Hedge Funds Need $300 Million in Assets Just to Break Even," Reuters, December 9, 2013). That's right, they make 2% per year plus 20% of all profits. So win or lose, hedge funds make big money for themselves regardless of whether the client does well or not!

But, hey, if you want to pay for the stuff that doesn't matter, then by all means go ahead and waste money on that crap – just please don't tell me you're getting better advice or products simply because you're rich. And make sure you keep your ego in check, because over-confidence goes hand-in-hand with greed, and greed can make you do some dumb things.

Speaking of ego, I have always found that men (myself included) need to fight harder than women to keep it in check. This will make it even harder for men to accept my suggestion to…

---

12 Source: Hedge Fund Research, Inc. (2018)

Chapter 15

Let the Woman Make the Decisions

"Man does not control his own fate;
the women in his life do that for him."
– Groucho Marx

One of the differences between men and women that I've observed in this business over the past twenty years or so is that **men tend to be more susceptible to fear and greed, the two primary emotions that pervade every aspect of finance, especially when it comes to the stock market**.

It is inevitably the husbands that call me to proclaim their new found wealth (even though it's just on paper) when the market is in a huge upswing, or to lament their loss (again, even though it's just on paper) when the stock market takes a big swing down. In short, men seem to be more fascinated by the daily, weekly, and monthly swings in the stock market (we men have got to admit the irony here, since we are the ones that accuse women of being too emotional!).

This phenomenon, where men may be more susceptible to their emotions when it comes to the markets, could be due to the fact that there seems to be more men than women gamblers. In fact, according to a huge study by the National Epidemiologic Survey on Alcoholism and Related Conditions (NESARC), pathological gambling is more common among men than women. And the stock and bond markets are, depending on your perspective, little more than huge casinos where people buy and sell securities.

That is exactly why I tell people who are looking for a profitable trade in a short period of time to head to Las Vegas instead – at least you get a free drink, and, oh by the way, the odds are probably more in your favor.

But I digress. The purpose of this chapter is not to deride men (which would actually be pretty stupid since I am a man), but rather highlight the fact that men, more so than women, may need to keep their emotions in check when making financial decisions.

Men would be well served by not only remembering that life is a journey rather than a destination, but also that investing is a marathon rather than a sprint. But men *and* women need to understand that the more emotions enter into financial decisions, the worse those decisions will be!

Speaking of emotional decisions, one of the toughest things to do is contemplate mortality. But the fact of the matter is that one day each of us is going to die, and the best thing we can do is focus on living in the moment, as well as never forgetting to plan for the future. This is why every man and woman needs to do some…

Chapter 16

Estate Planning

"Life is pleasant. Death is peaceful.
It's the transition that's troublesome."
– Isaac Asimov

It seems we are so busy taking care of life today, that we forget to prepare for tomorrow. As a financial planner and former attorney, part of my job is to help people craft a plan that not only looks at the present, but the future as well.

Toward that end, I recommend everyone create an estate plan that can help address the issues that arise if you become incapacitated or when you pass away. It doesn't matter if you are rich or poor, or young or old, there are several legal documents you should have just in case (and trust me, one day "just in case" will happen, as it does to everyone sooner or later).

The legal documents I recommend at a minimum include: will(s) and/or living trusts, durable general powers of attorney, healthcare powers of attorney, and living wills.

As everyone probably knows, a will basically says who gets what when you die. After you die, anything you owned will ultimately be distributed by the terms of your will (although it will need to go through the proper probate process, which means lawyers and courts, which in turn means fees and delays). If you pass away without a will, which is called intestate, then your state's laws will determine what happens to your estate (i.e., your stuff).

An alternative to a will is a revocable living trust. Although this trust essentially acts like a will by dictating who gets what, it does so through a different process that may help you avoid probate.

The reason why is simple: if you have titled something in the name of your living trust, then you don't own it when you die, and thus it avoids probate. Although this type of trust is really just a fiction while you are alive (since you are the trustee, have full control of the trust's assets, and can revoke the trust at any time), it can make things smoother for your heirs when you die.

However, there are a few things you need to be aware of. First, a trust may cost more time and money upfront. Second, a trust will not, in and of itself, help you avoid taxes. Sure, it can set up certain estate strategies to be utilized after you die, but a will can do the same thing. Unfortunately, some lawyers may tell prospective clients that a living trust will save them tax, but that's just not necessarily true.

The next legal document everyone should have is a general durable power of attorney. In short, this specifies who speaks for you if you cannot speak for yourself (if you're incapacitated).

It's "durable" in that the document survives even though you have become disabled or incompetent.

A health care power of attorney, which is called different things in different states (in some states it's called a "medical directive"), essentially specifies who can make medical decisions for you if you're unable.

Next, everyone should also have a living will, or advance directive. This document instructs your family and health care providers as to your wishes regarding medical treatment in the event you are unable to make those decisions. In contrast to the healthcare power of attorney, the living will is more specific as to what treatments, if any, you want utilized in life-threatening or life-prolonging situations.

The last document I strongly suggest all people create is a letter of instruction. Although a letter of instruction is not legally binding, this document can serve multiple purposes and help ease the burden on your heirs. One purpose is the identification of assets, where you list your assets and liabilities, what the account numbers are, how they are managed, etc.

Too frequently people die and leave their heirs little more than a paper trail to try and track down important assets (I actually knew a woman who found cash stashed in her deceased father's refrigerator eight months after he passed away). So you should also list the names and numbers of your current advisors, such as your lawyer, financial advisor, accountant, and clergy.

The letter of instruction should also mention your desired funeral arrangements. As morbid as it may sound to pre-plan for your death, the letter of instruction will help your surviving heirs at a time when they are feeling lost and trying to grieve.

All these documents can, and probably should, be prepared by a lawyer who has estate planning experience. However, I know people who are just as comfortable using an alternative provider such as LegalZoom.com to prepare these documents at a much lower cost. I cannot comment on taking one route or another, but I will say that either way you simply need to have something done.

Unfortunately, the most common decision people make is to do nothing, which is why things tend to be so messy when someone dies, and even more so when someone becomes incapacitated. I say "decision" because if you ignore planning for the inevitable, or claim to be too busy, then you have basically decided to saddle your family, friends, and/or the state with a hassle that they did not want, much less deserve.

So, if not for you, then do it for others – at least draft these simple documents. And while you're at it, do something else that may be worth more than any other document. Go ahead and write…

Chapter 17

Loving Letters

"Don't let it end like this; tell them I said something..."
— Pancho Villa's last words

While the primary focus of this book is to help you navigate your financial future, I feel that the following discussion, especially as it pertains to estate planning, is too important to overlook.

In fact, I believe a "loving letter" may be the most important estate planning document you can leave your loved ones. As I said before, life passes by too quickly, and we forget that our days here on earth are numbered. And what a tragedy it is when someone forgets or is unable to say goodbye before they leave this world. So the loving letter is your opportunity to say what you wanted to say before the inevitable occurs.

Simply write a letter or film a video, however long or short, to each person that is important to you. It can be to a husband or wife, a son or daughter, another family member, or even just a close friend. In this letter, you take the opportunity to tell them what you truly cherished about them. Write down some of those important, tender moments you had with them, and how they will never leave your heart after you have gone.

Let them know what was special about them and how much you cherished the time you had with them, or the memories they gave you. If you want to discuss specific instances or characteristics that warmed your heart, then do so. If you want to discuss your love for them in generalities, then do so. Either way, just make sure it comes from the heart. And please, please, **just write it down**.

I stress this because I have personally seen the power of a loving letter in action. Many years ago, after counseling a couple regarding estate planning, we discussed loving letters. In this case, I pushed a bit harder for them to write a loving letter to each of their three sons because, unfortunately, they had become estranged from one of those sons.

Long story made short, the husband died of cancer almost twelve months later. When I met with the family to help facilitate everything, the estranged son seemed the saddest of all.

When I asked him if he was all right, he said (as best my memory serves), "Tim, I never expected to receive a penny from my father, and so I am more than grateful that he left me some money. But I really don't care too much about the money – this means so much more to me." In his hand was the loving letter his father had written to him. In fact, years after his father passed, he still reads it when he is going through tough times.

So please, take the time to write a few loving letters. Because, so far as I know, we only get one chance at life here on Earth, and you do not want it to end without saying something!

Toward that end, I have one more thing to discuss. If money is the least bit important to you, then I have one last piece of advice, which is to...

Chapter 18

Do Your Homework & Take Action, or Suffer the Consequences

"Self-pity is our worst enemy, and if we yield to it, we can never do any good in the world."
– Helen Keller

By reading this book, you have demonstrated your interest in learning what action you can take; I congratulate you! But now you must follow up and actually take that action; you must take control and implement the ideas I have conveyed to you in this book.

So my last piece of advice is to actually challenge you. In fact, **I dare you to check up on me; see if what I have been telling you makes sense or can be substantiated through other sources, and then take action!**

You see, a little skepticism is good, and you can help yourself by being your own teacher. So don't just take my word for what I have taught you; do a little homework and see if you can confirm what I have told you. Because once you do, not only will you agree with most, if not all, of what I have told you, but all my points will be driven home – which in turn will hopefully push you to act upon all this great information.

But if you choose to ignore the information I have given you, then I wish you luck. Because there is an entire industry devoted to finance, and you can either use that industry to your advantage, or get run over by it.

Never forget that Wall Street is out to make money for Wall Street. And if you are too lazy or afraid to take control of the controllable variables, then you will get run over by Wall Street – and it will be your fault. So either do your homework and take action, or suffer the consequences.

If you do decide to take action and drive toward a more successful future, just remember that it is as easy as **1, 2, 3**:

One, keep Wall Street and yourself from causing harm; two, use common sense, especially when it comes to the tough issues; and three, Keep It $imple $tupid!

About the Author
R. Timothy Curran, JD, CFP®

Tim Curran is the founder and co-owner, along with his wife Wynne, of TWC Wealth Management in Charlotte, North Carolina; they are known as The Finance Couple™.

Tim graduated from the University of Texas at Austin, and then received his law degree from South Texas College of Law.

After a brief period of practicing law, Tim joined A.G. Edwards & Sons in 1996 and began working with individuals on comprehensive financial planning and asset management. In 2000, Tim joined UBS

Financial Services where he became a Vice President of Investments and earned his Senior Retirement Planning Consultant designation.

In 2003, Tim left UBS to become an independent advisor and start his own wealth management firm, focusing on personal financial planning and asset management.

Tim is a CERTIFIED FINANCIAL PLANNER™, a non-practicing attorney, an industry arbitrator for the southeast region of FINRA, and most importantly, a husband and father of two.

Made in the USA
Lexington, KY
20 September 2018